ZEUS-X-MECHANICA

Poems by Jason Ryberg

Kansas City Spartan Press Missouri

Spartan Press
Kansas City, Missouri
spartanpresskc.com

Spartan Press

Copyright (c) Jason Ryberg, 2017
First Edition 1 3 5 7 9 10 8 6 4 2
ISBN: 978-1-946642-08-0
LCC#: 2017900574

Design, edits and layout: Jason Ryberg, j.d.tulloch
Cover and author photo: Jon Bidwell
All rights reserved. No part of this publication may be reproduced or transmitted in any form or by any means, electronic or mechanical, including photocopying, recording or by info retrieval system, without prior written permission from the author.

Spartan Press would like to thank Prospero's Books, The Fellowship of N-finite Jest, The Prospero Institute of Disquieted P/o/e/t/i/c/s, Will Leathem, Tom Wayne, Jeanette Powers, j. d. tulloch, Jon Bidwell, Jason Preu, Mark McClane, Tony Hayden and the whole Osage Arts Community.

The author would like to thank the following publications in which some of these poems (in some form or another) originally appeared:

U City Review, Anti Heroin Chic, Trailer Park Quarterly, Ghoulish Intent, Kansas Time + Place, The Cape Rock, Indigent A La Carte, Blue Mountain Review, Rusty Truck, Kansas Time + Place, Prompts: A Spontaneous Anthology (39 West Press), Art Uprising (39 West Press), Ten Foot Tall And Bullet Proof (EMP), The Mutiny Information Reader (Mutiny Information Press, 2016),, The Gasconade Review: 39 Feet High and Rising, Your One Phone Call, Rye Whiskey Review, In Between Hangovers, Thimble Magazine, Ariel Chart

This book is dedicated to John and Melinda Ryberg.

CONTENTS

Still Life of Butterfly Perched on Clenched Fist (or, How's This for First Thought / Best Thought, Pt.1?) / 1

Zeus-X-Mechanica (or, Broken-Down Truck Stuck in the Weeds) / 2

A Day on the Farm, Pt. 1 / 4

Treehouse Fallen in the Backwoods / 5

Dead Man Watching Soap Operas / 7

Precious as Porcelain (or, Bathtub Virgin for a Shallow Grave) / 9

Ironic, Ain't It? / 11

Waking from a Nap at Dusk (Thinking That It's Morning) / 13

Sometimes the Moon is Nothing More Than the Moon / 15

Sitting in the Rain, Tit-Deep in the Gasconade River, Passing a Pint-Bottle of Evan Williams Back and Forth / 18

Dogs Gnawing Soup Bones on the Hard Wood Floor of Heaven / 20

The Island of Lost Personal Items and Effects / 23

9 Below Zero (or, the Who, What, Where, When, Why and How of It All) / 25

Hyper-Minimalist Poem with Title Longer Than Actual Poem Found in the Men's Room of a Stuckey's on I-25 Outside Chugwater, WY, Rendered in the Manner of Lawrence Ferlinghetti / 27

Space Girl for Earl / 28
Song of the Purple Impala (or,
   Bleeding Jesus on the Dashboard) / 29
Perhaps It Would Help
   if You Thought of the Poem as … / 30
Where-in It Tells Me, Night after Night,
   That It's Coming to Get Me / 32
Gardenias / 35
The Geometry of Need (or, How's This
   for First Thought / Best Thought, Pt. 2?) / 36
Opening Scenes From
   A Day in the Life of ... / 37
Poet in the Graveyard
   (Whistling *Dixie* in the Dark) / 40
Big Balls and All / 44
Lone Crow on a Telephone Pole / 45
The Sweet By and By (or,
   Curried Beef and Eggs
   for Breakfast) / 47
A Day on the Farm, Pt. 2 / 49
Watering the Tree of Reason with the
   Blood of Poets (or, How's This for
   First Thought / Best Thought Pt.3?) / 50
A List, Exhaustively Researched and Collated,
   of Everything That Could Even Be Conceivably
   Close (Under the Most Favorable Control
   Conditions) to Being Badder Than Bo Diddley / 51
Bloodhound with the Broke-Dick Blues / 52

*Look upon me, I'll show you
the life of the mind.*

—Karl *Madman* Mundt

Still Life of Butterfly Perched on Clenched Fist (or, How's This for First Thought / Best Thought, Pt.1?)

Woke up from a dream about something that seemed really important while it was happening, after having fallen asleep, apparently, in front of a fire in the backyard, only to suddenly wake, lost inside a prairie blizzard of fortune cookie fortunes, only to suddenly awake again, sitting upright in a rowboat that must have followed the moon out to sea while I was sleeping (again, apparently), only to bolt awake once more to a phone ringing and a strange voice on the other end asking me what my fortune said, whereupon I woke (finally, for real, this time, I think) in front of a pile of glowing embers with the urgent, frantic need to write down whatever it was that had come to me at the ground-zero / epicenter / inner onion eye of all these layers of dreams but all I could recover from the ocean floor refuse of it all was something about a butterfly perched on a clenched fist, closed around a handful of fortune cookie fortunes. Hell, I don't know, maybe it was a silver dollar or an earring. Maybe it was nothing.

Zeus-X-Mechanica (or, Broken-Down Truck Stuck in the Weeds)

> *Got no spare, got no jack, you don't give a shit*
> *you aint never goin' back.*
>
> -Tom Waits

Some days,
you feel like you've thrown a rod,

like all four tires have gradually gone flat,

like your body is riddled with rust and buckshot,

like there's a beehive in your glove-box
and a family of mice living in your guts
and you're OK with that,

like you're nothing more than
the quasi-poetic cliché of a broken-down truck
stuck in the weeds, by the side of a road
hardly anybody seems to use anymore,

a broken-down truck
abandoned right where it finally died
(finally gave up the automotive ghost for good,
this time), who knows how many years ago,
by someone who finally just said *fuck it*,
lit a cigarette and walked away

into the vast and starry planetarium
of just another night in America,
never to been seen
around these parts again.

Hell no.

Not if they could help it.

A Day on the Farm, Pt. 1

It would seem
that Billy the Goat
is seriously cogitating
on the all-too
tempting prospect
of bum-rushing me
and cows are honking
on the hillside
of early evening
and cars and trucks
are reeling out a distant
and near-constant hiss
and roar on the highway
just beyond the horizon
and then, *HO-leee Christ!*,
there's this huge Blue Heron
suddenly climbing
up from a stream
that runs through
the middle of the property,
not even thirty feet
away from me,
to the first current
of wind strong enough
to bear his weight up,
up and away he goes
(and in no particular
hurry).

Treehouse Fallen in the Backwoods

Kind of a curious thing
to come upon a fallen treehouse,
all of a sudden, in the deep Missouri backwoods
(somewhere in that hazy, uncharted zone
between North and South, noon and sundown);

one of those classic contemplative moments,
we could assume, that the universe
randomly puts in our paths, from time to time:

no other signs of civilization or human activity
of any kind for miles,

no reason one would even casually speculate
that a couple of wayward explorers could
randomly stumble upon such a scene
in an otherwise still reasonably untouched
and primeval forest setting like this,

no hoary, haggard Old Shepherd of the Hills
or prancing Tom Bombadil-like character
to spontaneously appear and tell us how
they've been here from the beginning,
how they've seen everything that's ebbed and
flowed through these parts since God was a baby,

no one who might have passively born witness
at that fateful isolated moment of entropic dissolution
(in the endless, Mobius loop of fateful moments
that this life of ours truly seems to be),

no one to answer what you would think
would be at least one of a number of obvious and
pressing questions* that would naturally come
to one's mind upon stumbling across a treehouse
that has fallen in the backwoods ...

A) What the hell?
B) Who built this thing?
C) Was anybody in it?
D) What's the sound of a treehouse falling in the woods?

Dead Man Watching Soap Operas

The irony wasn't so much
that a mummified corpse
was found reclining in a La-Z-Boy
in front of a television
with a soap opera playing
(one can imagine *Days of Our Lives*
or *As the World Turns,* maybe,
or even one of those spicy,
Telemundo telenovellas),
in an apartment building with
hundreds of other tenants,
coming and going all the time,
day and night, or that it actually
takes quite a bit of time and the right
environmental / atmospheric conditions,
they say, for a corpse to mummify
(as opposed to merely rot and liquefy)
or that the rent and utilities had
continued to be paid, automatically,
from a mysteriously bottomless
bank account for years and years,
or that the junk mail, at least,
must have kept piling up,
reliably, somewhere, or that
no one had apparently

come calling for any reason
in all that time (or if they did,
thought nothing of the television
being on at all hours, non-stop,
day and night) or what (if anything)
this whole thing says about us as a species or …

Wait … where was I going with this?

Precious as Porcelain (or, Bathtub Virgin for a Shallow Grave)

Heard she joined a convent somewhere in France or
>Spain when she was just a kid. Thought she
>wanted to be a saint or something.

Heard they were a front for the mob or the CIA or even
>the *Illuminati* (upon which so many routinely
>speculate and theorize late into the night).

Heard she got recruited into the inner circle of the
>organization to be trained as an elite,
>world-class assassin.

Heard the headmistress told her every day that she
>was as *precious as porcelain,* that she'd be perfect
>because no one would ever suspect her.

Heard that's the last thing you heard before everything
>went black, with a foot on your chest then
>two in the face: *why, you're just as precious
>as porcelain (POP! POP!).*

Heard she did that for twenty years, until one day
>it became one kill too many and she just
>walked away.

Heard she disappeared from it all, went on the run and
>off the grid of a murky underworld that was
>already off the grid.

Heard there was a price on her head.
Heard there were sightings in Mogadishu, Bangladesh
    and Bangor, Maine, even.
Heard anyone who went looking was never
    heard from again.
Heard some hotshot looking to make a name
    got a hot tip.
Heard this fool came calling one day, looking for blood
    or to claim the bounty or maybe even try to
    pull her back into *the life* for just one last big score.
Heard she invited him in for cucumber sandwiches
    and a fine darjeeling and a little talk about
    the weather, and now that sorry son of a bitch
    is buried in her backyard garden,
    in a shallow grave beneath a bathtub virgin,
    feeding the worms and microbes
    and thirsty shoots and rootlets
    of Marigolds, Tulips and Daylilies …

Precious as porcelain.

Ironic, Ain't It?

that,
>   while constantly
>>   being re-reminded
>   by the representatives
>>   of forces
(presumably)

>   larger than ourselves,
from time
>   to time
>>   to time, of one's (seemingly

>   pre-ordained and inescapable)
>>   holding place
in whatever
>   grand (or even less than
>   grand) schemata of peoples /
>>   places / things
>   you happen to currently find yourself
steeped in,
>   is indeed sobering, it also,
>>   (maybe not-so) oddly enough,
>   in turn, makes the notion

of pulling several monster
>>   rippers

                              off a bong
      made from an adorably
                        google-eyed
                           ceramic bunny and
             sipping on a quadruple
                              Americano
            while flipping
                        back and forth between
        a (sur)reality show about
                          Amish gangsters and
      bat-shit religious programming
                           on the local access channel,
            sound like just as good
                              a way as any
                                    to start
                  the day.

Waking from a Nap at Dusk (Thinking That it's Morning)

One of those naps
where you lay your
head on the pillow with
the honest-to-god intent
of just catching maybe
20 or 30 minutes, *max*,
but instead end up
plunging right through
the bed and tumbling,
top hat over tap shoe,
down, down, down
a deep, ancient dark well
of weird Freudian /
Jungian dreams (where
in every one you're
never wearing any pants,
for some reason) and
then suddenly pop
out the other end
of 1, 2, 3, maybe
even 4 hours
later in near-
total darkness,

wondering
who, what,
where,
when,
why and
how
the
fuck!?

Sometimes the Moon is Nothing More Than the Moon

Sometimes the moon comes down
(if she happens to be in town)
from her royal couch of clouds
to drink with us (my shadow
and me) when no one else will.

Sometimes the moon rings like a temple bell
on a brittle, breathless, freeze-dried night,
signaling the beginning (or maybe the end)
of something important and radiates
with a halo of steam like a luminous
ball of dry ice.

Sometimes the moon is a curved dagger
that some Bedouin bandit prince
might have brandished in the blue and grainy
late, late show of my childhood dreams.

Sometimes the moon is a white rose
that drunken fools inevitably try
to shoot arrows and poems at,
knowing full-well that both return
to Earth with potentially dangerous results.

Sometimes the moon is a pallid face
peering in at us through a Winter window scene
while the radio begins to glow with a moody
Ellington *Indigo* and a car down on the street
is struggling to clear the early frost from its throat.

Sometimes the moon is a cop's
flashlight cutting a cautious path
through film-noir ghosts of gutter steam.

Sometimes the moon is a 60-watt bulb
shining from the back porch,
out into the sweaty, firefly-infused,
backyard jungle nights of long ago.

Sometimes the moon is a guard tower spot,
always trying to catch us with its magic lasso
whenever we make our midnight raids, over the walls,
into the Garden of Earthly Delights.

Sometimes the moon is a silver dollar
that's been sheared in two by a dull
and rusty pair of tin snips.

Sometimes the moon is a shiny dime
flattened on a railroad track,
in which, if one looks just right,
a semblance of Roosevelt's confident
and reassuring smirk can still be seen.

Sometimes the moon is a fat, blue
androgynous Buddha, grinning out
at the universe in every direction at once.

Sometimes the moon is a single bright eye
of a dark god of the ancient world,
peering down at us through a hole torn
in the top of a circus tent of clouds,
or up from an inversely alternate underworld
through the dimensional portal
of a swollen, marshy pond.

Sometimes the moon is nothing more
than the moon.

No.

That's never true.

Sitting in the Rain, Tit-Deep in the Gasconade River, Passing a Pint-Bottle of Evan Williams Back and Forth

for Jeanette Powers

The river has been stirred up a bit
by this low-level, end-of-summer shower
and keeps attempting to sweep us
and our bottle away downstream
to wash up who-knows-where.

But our butts are too firmly planted
in the rocks, here, our conversation
too deeply delved into for us
to surrender so easily, now.

Leaves and sticks float by.

A lone Blue Heron
wings and *skronks* its way,
across the river and over the trees
on the other side.

Dragonflies dance their crazy
electric calligraphy along
the water's surface.

Tiny stones *rat-a-tat* and *clickity-click*
their Morse code / ticker-tape
network on the muddy bottom.

The bottle goes back and forth.

Rain continues
to fall.

Dogs Gnawing Soup Bones on the Hard Wood Floor of Heaven

No, that's not thunder,
that's dogs gnawing soup bones
on the hard wood floor of heaven.

No, those aren't dogs,
those are dragons wolfing down the clouds
and shitting them back out.

No, those aren't bones,
those are the balustrades of mountains,
finally cracking and giving way
from holding up the weight of the sky for so long.

No, that's not a wood floor,
that's the tin roof of a rat-infested shit-house
in the boggy backwoods of Mississippi.

No, that's not the backwoods,
that's the back-40 of an abandoned farm
being slowly reclaimed by time
and a primordial swamp that's haunted
by the ghosts of slaves who never made it North.

No, those aren't ghosts,
those are gusts of wind
carrying the words of people a world away.

No, that's not the wind,
that's all the forests of the world
inhaling and exhaling in unison.

No, those aren't forests of trees,
those are armies of the skeletons of giants
that once walked the earth, waiting for the wind
to bring them the words that will finally
wake them up again.

No, those aren't skeletons, those are structural profiles
for buildings of an alien and non-Euclidian
architecture that began construction long before
humans ever walked up-right.

No, those aren't prototype *homo erecti,*
those are bears, owls, coyotes walking through
the sleeping suburbs at night,
wearing their human skins.

No, those aren't the suburbs,
those are future ruins and landfills
built on the ancient burial grounds
of the first Americans.

No, those aren't burial grounds,
those are the resting places
of forgotten gods and monsters
of the ancient world, dreaming of the days
when they were the top of the food chain.

No, that's not the fitful stirring of
gods and monsters in their sleep,

it's just a little thunder.

The Island of Lost Personal Items and Effects

He told us he came from the Island
of Lost Personal Items and Effects
and handed me an ancient cigar box
lined and padded with crumpled receipts
and scraps of scratch-paper with phone numbers
and addresses hastily scrawled on them.

In it were nested keys, gloves, driver's licenses, sunglasses,
and three fairly expensive-looking Zippo lighters.
Whenever he closed and reopened the lid,
different items would be contained inside:
pens, cell-phones and wedding rings, earrings
and cufflinks, pocket-knives and pocket-watches.

He carried a fancy oriental parasol
which he claimed gave him the power of flight
and wore hip-waders which he said allowed him
to stroll freely around in the fabled River of Time
as often as he liked (and with little fear
of being pulled under and swept away
by its notorious undercurrents).

He also had an old cane pole
strung with telegraph wire which he baited with
glittering baby dreams to lure variations of the *Truth*
(in all its slippery countenances and for his own
personal and unspecified use, I would assume).

The candlelight in our kitchen made his shadow
dance a curious dance along the opposite wall and
made his face seem like the face of a grinning
bone china Buddha.

When he got up to leave he stopped and said to us,
*I wouldn't put too many of my eggs (golden or
otherwise) in with planets and stars, nor with lucky
numbers and fortunes, no more than I would
on dogs and horses ...*

We never saw him again.

9 Below Zero (or, the Who, What, Where, When, Why and How of It All)

9 Below Zero don't care who you are,
who you know or who your daddy is.

9 below zero don't care what you think,
what you want or what your astrological sign is.

9 below zero don't care where you come from,
where you did your master's thesis
or where you're in such a hurry to be.

9 below zero don't care when your birthday is,
when the rent is due or even when
the end of the world is coming.

9 below zero don't care why you're here,
why you think you deserve only the best things in life
or why you act the way you do sometimes.

9 below zero don't care how much money you make,
how you make your money or how much your
wrist-watch cost.

No, 9 below zero don't give a damn about the who,
what, where, when, why and how of it all,

because 9 below zero
is 9 below zero,

and falling …

Hyper-Minimalist Poem with Title Longer Than Actual Poem Found in the Men's Room of a Stuckey's on I-25 Outside Chugwater, WY, Rendered in the Manner of Lawrence Ferlinghetti

You

done

fucked-

up

now,

son.

Space Girl for Earl

She's lean, she's mean, her skin is green, she looks like the girl of Captain Kirk's dreams. She got big blue eyes, she got big blue hair, she causes public scenes with the clothes she wears. SPACE GIRL! FOR EARL! SPACE GIRL! FOR EARL! She's a beehive baby, a rockin' rocket queen, she digs Chuck Berry and a quart of Clear Springs. If you think you've seen it all, well, man you haven't, she's a voodoo love goddess from another planet. SPACE GIRL! FOR EARL! SPACE GIRL! FOR EARL! Oh yeah, she got antenna stickin' outta her head, her teeth are pearly white, her lips are ruby red, she was crankin' Jay Hawkins when we saw her land and she said she plays bass in a space girl band. SPACE GIRL! FOR EARL! SPACE GIRL! FOR EARL! The next thing she said was, *I wanna know if this here's the place where all the hepcats go.* Then she said, *Daddy-O, don't be no square, I'll teach you a step that'll curl your hair.* SPACE GIRL! FOR EARL! SPACE GIRL! FOR EARL! Platform boots and shiny clothes, where she comes from noone knows. She hit the gas and she was gone, gone, gone. Her license plate said *FROM BEYOND.* SPACE GIRL FOR EARL! SPACE GIRL FOR EARL! SPACE GIRL FOR EARL! SPACE GIRL FOR EARL! SPACE GIRL FOR EARL! SPACE GIRL FOR EARL! SPACE GIRL FOR EARL! SPACE GIRL FOR EARL! SPACE GIRL FOR EARL! SPACE GIRL FOR EARL! SPACE GIRL FOR EARRRLLLL!!!

Song of the Purple Impala (or, Bleeding Jesus on the Dashboard)

He swears that it came with the car
when he bought it from the old man
with the wooden leg, out off Old-40 HWY
*(I am crappin' you negative, son,
a goddamn wooden leg)*, that he wasn't
particularly religious but thought it might
bring him a little luck on his midnight runs,
back and forth, across the state line:
a '68 purple Impala complete with its own
fuzzy dice and bleeding Jesus on the dashboard,
though he always maintained that
he kept it tuned-up and tight and had
the latest police scanners and fuzz-busters
(this is back before they could detect you
detecting them, mind you) and a USMC
and I SUPPORT THE HIGHWAY PD
stickers on the rear bumper (*Christ,
those dumbass hippies with their peace signs
and Grateful Dead shit just askin' to get
pulled-over*), and, that the actual moment
of stigmata would only occur (if you
believe in such things) when you got it
cranked up to 100-plus, and if anybody
doubted him and ever wanted to witness
this theological miracle for themselves,
why, hell, he'd gladly take them for a drive.
Anytime.

Perhaps it Would Help
if You Thought of the Poem as …

a hermit's hovel of many mansions,

a shimmering silk kimono billowing
on a clothes line in central Kansas,

a meteorite, suddenly fallen in your backyard
(pulsing with a strangely hypnotic
and inviting glow),

a particularly toxic strain of word virus,

a flashbulb moment of clarity
in the middle of a moshpit,

a tattered travelogue entry written in hobo code,

a series of lies that leads (ultimately) to (something
resembling) the (big time, capital *T*) Truth,

a random, haphazard arrangement
of the 10,000 myriad archetypes of the world,

a sum of parts that is somehow actually larger
than its whole,

an unexpected arrival at reality
via the unwitting disengagement from it,

an open-air market bazaar in a lost city,

a Chinese puzzle box or Russian nesting doll,
flowering open and open, forever down and down
the spiraling, helical dog-tail chase for the Good,
the Just and the Beautiful, etc, etc.

Or, perhaps it would help if you thought of this
fragile little contraption of memes as a mechanical
butterfly flittering the non-Euclidian geometry
of its flight pattern through a forest of wind-chimes,
still glistening with rain from a brief
morning thundershower.

Where-in It Tells Me, Night after Night, That It's Coming to Get Me

for Thad Haverkamp

On the first night, at the foot of the stairs,
It said It was a strain of light refracted from
the Universal Pilot Light they say is somewhere
deep inside every one of us (at times, little more
than a firefly (they say) struggling Its way
through a dense *purgatorio* of smog and doubt).
Oh, and something about coming to get me.

On the second night, on the second step,
It said It was the often conspicuous
and unpredictable absence of hope
(that red-headed, hair-lipped little step-child
of the world). And, that It was definitely
coming to get me.

On the third night, on the third step,
It said It was a chest full of confederate money,
found clutched-up in the gnarled roots
of an old willow tree, outside Gnaw Bone, IN.
And, not to worry, that It was still coming to get me.

On the fourth night, on the fourth step,
It said It was a bust of Hank Williams (Sr.,
of course) that some people swear cries
tears of blood every Mother's Day.
And, that It was just kidding.
It wasn't really coming to get me.

On the fifth night, on the fifth step,
It said It was a brief and unexpected Summer rain,
the kind that happens on days when the skies are
blue and clear and the sun is shining. And, that I
must be really stupid or something.
Of course, It was still coming to get me.

On the sixth night, on the sixth step,
It said It was white sheets billowing
and snapping on a clothesline and a flock
of waterfowl suddenly startled into flight.
And, It wanted to know what I was wearing.

On the seventh night, on the seventh step,
It said It was the fateful phone call
at 4am that no one wants to answer:
ring-ring, ring-ring, Hey, it's me, I'm almost there!

On the eighth night, on the eighth step,
It said It was the last peach of the season,
waiting to finally fall from the limb. And,
did I get the package that It sent?

On the ninth night, on the ninth step,
It said It was an old Spiderman lunchbox
full of strange keys and foreign coins.
And, how did I feel about the films of Wes Anderson?

On the tenth night, on the tenth step,
It said It was a blind river flowing beneath the prairie
as well as the herd of bison above it. And, It wanted
to know why they called them *buffalo wings.*

On the eleventh night, on the eleventh step,
It said It was the lone, melancholy comedian of a crow,
cackling its tired routine on a scarecrow's hapless shoulder.
And, had I heard the one about the priest,
the rabbi and the donkey who walk into a bar mitzvah?

On the twelfth night, just outside my bedroom door,
It said It was a jelly jar full of fireflies. And, that with
all do respect, It generally preferred Dio-era Sabbath.

And finally, on the thirteenth night,
at the foot of the bed,
It said …

> *Seriously, dude, what's the fuckin' hold up?*
> *We got work to do.*

Gardenias

This night, like any other lonesome,
wide-open night down here on this
mean, old mortally coiled-up world of ours.

These rather cruel and unresponsive stars
staring right through us all the time
with the cold, indifferent light of their million-
upon-million light year stares.

The empty, unfathomably chasmic spaces
in between them, between them and me,
and each one of them actually a sun
with some kind of planetary system
of its own, they say.

And for some reason (don't ask me why),
it all leaves me thinking of that scene
in *Apocalypse Now* where Brando is talking
to Sheen about some abandoned and overgrown
gardenia plantation on the banks of the Ohio River—

> *like five miles of heaven just opened up on the Earth*
> *in the form of gardenias.*

Weird, huh.

The Geometry of Need (or, How's this for First Thought / Best Thought, Pt. 2?)

Sometimes it seems that some folks absolutely need some sort of Ptolemaically structured pantheon of varying shades and degrees, pie-graphs and Venn-diagrams of Xs, Ys and Zs symbolizing, charting and compartmentalizing all the various diametrically opposing dichotomies of devils and gods, demons and angels, aristocrats and street-sweepers, embrace-ables and untouchables, lowly princes and lordly paupers. Yes, indeed, sometimes it seems that some folk's days (hell, their very lives, I tell you!) would not be complete without something to sneer at juxt-opposed against something to lustfully leer at, something to loathe and something to fetishize, something to suckle up to and something to demonize from on-high, and seriously ... what the hell is wrong with you people!?

Opening Scenes From
A Day in the Life of ...

*Exterior. Morning. A farm somewhere in the Midwest.
Late Fall or early Winter.*

First, there is the angry hornet's buzz
of the alarm clock, followed by
the sacred ritual of the snooze button.

Down in the kitchen,
a hyper-modern coffee machine
automaticly begins to mumble and whisper to itself
like old, worn-out plumbing while the news of the world
trickles out from an ancient radio (fifty years, at least).

The light over the sink
is an ice-blue flare floating in stasis
above the landscape of last night's dishes.

Outside, the world is covered-over
with a brittle, glassy layer of ice
that will most likely be gone before noon.

The sharp, black silhouettes of trees, telephone poles
and a lone silo begin to define themselves against
the glowing backdrop of a pink and mother-of -pearl
swath of cloud that's arching out over the horizon line
like the crest of a tidal wave or a distant mountain range.

Meanwhile, the yard has suddenly filled
with the chatter and rustle
of a roving theater troupe of crows.

They strut and mill and gossip about the yard
and drive, a few perched upon the front porch railing,
the naked limbs of the Linden trees and all along
the neighbor's Classic American White Picket Fence,

even one lone fellow pacing and pecking about
in the middle of the road:

a motley convention of lowbrow critics
and (off-)color commentators laying open
this small, unremarkable part of the world
to their sharp, shrill scrutiny.

The scene officially ends with the slamming
of a screen door and an island of black feathers
suddenly exploding into the sky.

The next one thunders to a start
with the turning of a key.

What awaits our unsuspecting protagonist
as the first tentative thread of plot leads him deeper
up-river into the dark interior of the story?

Alien invasion?
Zombie hordes?
Terrorist attack?
Hostage situation?

Or, maybe just a low-budget,
art-house bro-mantic comedy
with a cast of mostly unknowns
(and maybe a few obligatory A-list cameos),

the kind they just don't
seem to make anymore,

about another
day in the life of ...

Fade to black.

Opening credits start to roll.

Indie rock music begins to play.

Poet in the Graveyard
(Whistling *Dixie* in the Dark)
for Brandon Whitehead

It was mid-July
and had rained most of the day
(so you can bet your ass it was humid
and sticky as hell) and I had this goofy tune
bouncing around inside my head
that I just couldn't shake: *way down yonder
in the land of cotton, old times there,
they aint forgotten, look away,
look away, look away ...*

You know the one.

And the moon and the stars
were nowhere to be seen
and the locusts and the crickets
had their maniacal cartoon calliope machines
cranked all the way to *eleven.*

And I was seriously entertaining the idea
of turning the hell around
and taking the long way home
WHEN SUDDENLY! (and aint it always
suddenly in situations like this?)

I found one of my feet sunk knee-deep
in what I soon realized was a very recently filled
(very recently rained-upon) burial plot.

And the moon and the stars
were still refusing to show
and I'd swear my spook show
accompaniment of crickets and locusts
came to an absolute dead stop.

And yes, I believe I very nearly soiled myself
(very nearly *filled my britches*
as my Uncle Mikey used to say)
as I sprawled and struggled, there,
in the oily, mucky, mosquito-infused dark.

And sure, I'd like to say that's how they found me
(the groundskeepers, the cops,
the EMTs, whoever),

that I was babbling and raving wildly
and had obviously gone mad,
my hair turned completely white, even,
that I'd clawed my own eyes out at the sight
of some horrible thing that
just should not be,

that something down there
had grabbed my leg and pulled
and pulled (not totally dissimilar
from the way you may think
I've been pulling yours, I'm sure),

that I've written this whole thing
while resting and recuperating, *indefinitely,*
under strict observation at a minimum security
mental health facility (in that classic
Lovecraftian fashion).

But no,
eventually I *Christ-all-mightied,*
rat-fuck-bastard'
and *son-of-a-bitched* my foot free
just as it began to rain again.

And, eventually,
I collected my scattered faculties
and somehow summoned the desperate,
drunken courage to reach down deep
into that slimy suck-hole and retrieve my shoe
(now, pretty much ruined),
then shamefully shambled
and squelched my way home.

And all the while,
that sinister and perverse musical phantom
pin-balling around inside the empty
Victorian opera-house of my skull,
tormenting me with its cloying,
insipid adulation for the Lost Confederate Cause
and the grand old antebellum South...

But I'd be goddamned if I was gonna give
whatever smug and smirking gods looking
down on me the satisfaction,

no matter how goddamn catchy
that goddamed tune was.

Big Balls and All

Some days even the dirty backsides
of old buildings have a sort of disheveled
and crumbling beauty to them
like neatly stacked heaps of scrap
with sagging fire escapes and cracked,
wire-mesh windows bursting forth
with clots of bird's nests, here and there:
a small, man-made mountain range
piled against a sweeping backdrop
of clouds like drifting glacial masses
and the sky all atomic swimming pool blue.
And here, grazing in the foreground
on the south side of Larry's Auto Supply,
looking like it could have been painted yesterday,
the bull of an old Bull Durham Tobacco sign
(big balls and all), recently uncovered, I'm told
by some old boy in bib over-alls and muddy boots
(with the steel toes showing through),
when the building next to it got hit by lightning
last month and burned down. *Other than that*,
he says, *been a pretty quiet summer.*

Lone Crow on a Telephone Pole

Certainly a lone crow
perched on a telephone pole
at a foggy country cross-roads
at 7:37 on a Monday morning
in mid-October must be
some kind of sign,
some kind of portent or
hoodoo or sinister hex,
some kind of harbinger
of impending doom that
is starting to resemble,
(ever)more and (ever)more,
Poe's imposing raven
sitting on its bust of Palas,
'specially since the son-
of-a-bitch won't do anything
but squat there and stare down
at you, no matter how
many times you honk
your horn, flip him the bird,
and mutter out, *Oh yeah?*
Well fuck you too!,
because despite all your
alleged hard-wired,
country boy, backroads
sensibilities, you're the one
who somehow keeps

making all these stupid
wrong turns that keep
returning you, again
and again, to the same
(presumably inhospitable)
place you started from.

Not him.

Fool.

The Sweet By and By (or, Curried Beef and Eggs for Breakfast)

for Tony Hayden

The only answer, really,
to a morning after a night
of too much curried beef and bourbon
is, of course, more bourbon
and maybe some brown sugar
(if you have it) mixed into a mug
of hot, tar-black coffee,

an old tattered bathrobe,
an even older folding chair,
a pair of cheap sunglasses (seriously,
never pay more than ten bucks
because, sure-as-shit, you'll lose them
or sit on them or something equally
catastrophic),

a book of *800 Years of Ancient Chinese Poetry,* a cool(-ish),
moody wind in the spindly,
spider web trees (strung, here
and there, with invisible chimes
it seems),

a smelly mutt named Murph
or Zeus or Lucky to bring you
a stick to throw, from time to time,

left-over curried beef
and eggs (over-easy)
warming on the stove,

a muddy river sliding
lazily, by and by, and there,
in the distance, a rustic,
country Charon, maybe,
ferrying some recently
departed soul on over
to the other side.

A Day on the Farm, Pt. 2

A grackle perched on a fence post
beneath an electric blue sky
where mountains and fat landmasses of cloud
do their continental drift thing.

Tiny sets of wings,
blue, yellow, orange,
like the petals of wildflowers,
flutter up from the grass.

The wind and the trees are twisting
(like they did last summer
and who knows how many summers before).

A sparrow is sitting on the driver's
side mirror of a beat-to-shit pick-up truck
in the middle of a clump of grass and weeds
grown conspicuously tall
on a small square of the property
where all else is kept fairly low
to the ground.

Keys still in the ignition.
Battery still good.
Radio works.

Motherfuckin' Chuck Berry.

Watering the Tree of Reason with the Blood of Poets (or, How's this for First Thought / Best Thought Pt.3?)

With wings I stitched together from silk pillowcases, sheets and lady's lacey underthings (pinched, admittedly, from a country clothes-line or three), I sit here, once again, waiting (in the wings) for the wind to draw a big breath up, up, up from its deepest, most sub-subterranean wells and bellows (down, down, <small>down</small> where the only light to speak of emits from phosphorescent gems and jewels, which, we can, of course, remote view with the invisible and buoyant looking-glass of the poem) and blow, man, blow and then O-U-W-T OUWT! I go into The Big Wide Open, out into The Big Who Knows, out into The Big Nowhere / Everywhere / Anywhere / Whereever / Whatever, I'm gone, gone, gone ... And should these wings of my maiden flight (from the maddening plight of constant and futile border-warring and inner-skirmishes of attrition), instead, fail and this Hefty Bag of bones and meat I call my body, my me, my very being, flail and drop like a load-stone, Wile E. Coyote style, would it really be so bad if the blood (if not just the sweat, piss and tears) of this on-again / off-again ex-patriot / armchair philosopher / one-note poetaster watered, one last time, the roots of the tree of reason?

A List, Exhaustively Researched and Collated, of Everything That Could Even Be Conceivably Close (Under the Most Favorable Control Conditions) to Being Badder Than Bo Diddley

1)

2)

3)

4)

5)

6)

7)

8)

9)

10)

Bloodhound with the Broke-Dick Blues

As in it don't work so good no more.

As in *it* could clearly be a metaphor
for any number of vital physical or even
meta-physical components.

As in maybe we are and maybe we aren't really
talking about a bloodhound, here, right?

As in a man sometimes just misses doing the things
he can't do as well as he used to like some kind of
goddamn phantom limb syndrome.

As in sometimes all that excess *anima* just builds and
builds until it can't hold to the center, or the center,
itself, suddenly just cannot maintain its structural
integrity.

As in sometimes when the stars are properly aligned
or the moon is just right and the jar of moonshine
you been nipping on all night is starting to talk
to you, you just can't keep it under wraps any longer.

As in that moon and those stars and that hooch are
clearly messing with you, boy, challenging you, in fact,
flat-out double-dog daring you to free the dragon
from the root-cellar, let the monkeys out of the attic
and shake the fireflys from your hair.

As in you have to put the call out right now to all the
    freight trains and coyotes in your immediate vicinity
    or something's gonna give, something gonna blow,
    something gonna burn the goddamn saw-mill down.

As in this just might be the night to finally call both
    God and the Devil out to their respective front
    porches and find out once and for all why both those
    mendacious sons-o-bitches have restraining orders
    placed against you.

As in it might be time to do some truth-tellin, some
    eye-witnessing, some sanctifying, some hard core
    preachin' and prophesying.

As in this deep-down ache needs to be acknowledged
    and validated, this sorrowful soul exonerated,
    purged and redeemed by a little one-on-one,
    call and response session with the universe.

As in someone on the other end needs to pick-up,
    right now!

As in this just might finally be the night
    to flap these goddamned floppity bloodhound ears
    and fly, fly away, motherfuckers,
    fly, fly away ...

Jason Ryberg is the author of fourteen books of poetry, six screenplays, a few short stories, several angry letters to various magazine and newspaper editors, and a box full of folders, notebooks and scraps of paper that could one day be (loosely) construed as a novel. He is currently an artist-in-residence at both The Prospero Institute of Disquieted P/o/e/t/i/c/s and the Osage Arts Community. He lives part-time in Kansas City with a rooster named Little Red and a billygoat named Giuseppe and part-time somewhere in the Ozarks, near the Gasconade River, where there are also many strange and wonderful woodland critters.

The cover photos for this series were contributed by Jon Bidwell, a photographer who lives and works in Kansas. To view more of his work, visit him at www.instagram.com/jonbidwell.

This project was made possible, in part, by generous support from the Osage Arts Community.

Osage Arts Community provides temporary time, space and support for the creation of new artistic works in a retreat format, serving creative people of all kinds — visual artists, composers, poets, fiction and nonfiction writers. Located on a 152-acre farm in an isolated rural mountainside setting in Central Missouri and bordered by ¾ of a mile of the Gasconade River, OAC provides residencies to those working alone, as well as welcoming collaborative teams, offering living space and workspace in a country environment to emerging and mid-career artists. For more information, visit us at www.osageac.org

Osage Arts Community

www.ingramcontent.com/pod-product-compliance
Lightning Source LLC
Chambersburg PA
CBHW021452080526
44588CB00009B/804